THE
LOVE & *GRATITUDE*
NOTEBOOK

FULMAR OXFORD PUBLISHERS,
OXFORD, UNITED KINGDOM

The Love & Gratitude Notebook
200 lined pages with 100 inspiring quotes, Gratitude Boxes & Love Notes
[Cover color: Royal Blue]

Cover designed by Andjela K.
Copyright © 2019

The Love & Gratitude Notebook Collection

 editor@fulmaroxford.com

 @FulmarOxford

 /fulmaroxford

Visit us at www.fulmaroxford.com

A Note from the Editor

Whether you are using this notebook for school, for work, or for journaling, it was designed with two specific needs in mind:

1. The need to express how grateful you are, each day, for all the blessings in your life.
2. The need to feel loved and to express love every day.

Gratitude and love are the cornerstones of The Law of Attraction and the principles of Abundance. The more you feel and express them, the more opportunities you get to do so.

The *Gratitude* boxes in this notebook are designed for you to express how grateful you feel regarding the people in your life, God, the Universe, a pet—whomever or whatever comes to your mind.

In the *Note of Love* sections, you may express your love for anyone and anything. For example: "*I love Mom. She makes a great breakfast.*" Or: "*I love the river because it improves my mood!*"

As you go about your daily journey, we hope that you will benefit from this notebook in many ways, and that it will bring lots of joy, gratitude and love into your life.

"Let us rise up and be thankful, for if we didn't learn a lot today, at least we learned a little, and if we didn't learn a little, at least we didn't get sick, and if we got sick, at least we didn't die; so, let us all be thankful."

—Buddha

Date: _____   **Time:** _____

"A grateful mind is a great mind which eventually attracts to itself great things."
—Plato

3 things I am grateful for today:	A Note of Love for...
1).	
2).	
3).	

Date: _____   **Time:** _____

"There is no fear in love; but perfect love casteth out fear..."
(*Holy Bible*, 1 John 4:18 / King James Version)

3 things I am grateful for today:	A Note of Love for...
1).	
2).	
3).	

Date: _____   **Time:** _____

"Do not spoil what you have by desiring what you have not; remember that what you now have was once among the things you only hoped for."
—Epicurus

3 things I am grateful for today:	A Note of Love for...
1).	
2).	
3).	

Date: _____ **Time:** _____

"My little children, let us not love in word, neither in tongue; but in deed and in truth."
(*Holy Bible*, 1 John 3:18 / King James Version)

3 things I am grateful for today:	A Note of Love for...
1).	
2).	
3).	

Date: _____ **Time:** _____

"Beloved, let us love one another: for love is of God..."
(*Holy Bible*, 1 John 4:7 / King James Version)

3 things I am grateful for today:	A Note of Love for...
1).	
2).	
3).	

Date: _____ **Time:** _____

"…love one another: for he that loveth another hath fulfilled the law."
(*Holy Bible*, Romans 13:8 / King James Version)

3 things I am grateful for today:	A Note of Love for...
1).	
2).	
3).	

"He who is filled with love is filled with God himself."
—Saint Augustine

3 things I am grateful for today:	A Note of Love for...
1).	
2).	
3).	

"The reward of goodness is nothing but goodness."
(Holy Qur'an 55:61)

3 things I am grateful for today:	A Note of Love for...
1).	
2).	
3).	

Date: _____   **Time:** _____

"I love them that love me; and those that seek me early shall find me."
(*Holy Bible,* Proverbs 8:17 / King James Version)

3 things I am grateful for today:	A Note of Love for...
1).	
2).	
3).	

Date: _____ Time: _____

"When I am with you, we stay up all night. When you're not here, I can't go to sleep. Praise God for those two insomnias! And the difference between them."
—Rumi

3 things I am grateful for today:	A Note of Love for...
1).	
2).	
3).	

Date: _____ Time: _____

"That possession which we gain by the sword is not lasting; gratitude for benefits is eternal."
—Quintus Curtius Rufus (*De Rebus Gestis Alexandri Magni*, Act VIII, Scene 8)

3 things I am grateful for today:	A Note of Love for...
1).	
2).	
3).	

Date: _____ **Time:** _____

"There are only two ways to live your life. One is as though nothing is a miracle. The other is as though everything is a miracle."
—Albert Einstein

3 things I am grateful for today:	A Note of Love for...
1).	
2).	
3).	

«Porque la esperanza siempre nace al mismo tiempo que el amor.»
"…for hope is always born at the same time as love…"
—Miguel de Cervantes *(Don Quixote)*

3 things I am grateful for today:	A Note of Love for...
1).	
2).	
3).	

Date: _____ **Time:** _____

"God always rewards gratitude."
(*Holy Qur'an* 4:147 / Abdul Haleem translation)

3 things I am grateful for today:	A Note of Love for...
1).	
2).	
3).	

Date: _____ **Time:** _____

"And whatsoever ye do in word or deed, do all in the name of the Lord Jesus,
giving thanks to God and the Father by him."
(*Holy Bible*, Colossians 3:17 / King James Version)

3 things I am grateful for today:	A Note of Love for...
1).	
2).	
3).	

Date: _____ **Time:** _____

"Love will not be constrain'd by mastery [...] Love is a thing as any spirit free."
—Geoffrey Chaucer (*The Canterbury Tales*)

3 things I am grateful for today:	A Note of Love for...
1).	
2).	
3).	

Date: _____ **Time:** _____

"For of him, and through him, and to him [...] be glory forever."
(*Holy Bible*, Romans 11:36 / King James Version)

3 things I am grateful for today:	A Note of Love for...
1).	
2).	
3).	

Date: _____   **Time:** _____

"God loves each of us as if there were only one of us."
—Saint Augustine

3 things I am grateful for today:	A Note of Love for...
1).	
2).	
3).	

Date: _____   Time: _____

"I was not yet in love, yet I loved to love...I sought what I might love, in love with loving."
—Saint Augustine

3 things I am grateful for today:	A Note of Love for...
1).	
2).	
3).	

Date: _____   **Time:** _____

"And over all these virtues put on love, which binds them all together in perfect unity."

(*Holy Bible*, Colossians 3:14 / New International Version)

3 things I am grateful for today:	A Note of Love for...
1).	
2).	
3).	

Date: _____   **Time:** _____

"I will love those who love me, and those who seek me eagerly will find me."
(*Holy Tanakh* - Proverbs 8:17)

3 things I am grateful for today:	A Note of Love for...
1).	
2).	
3).	

"When I despair, I remember that all through history the way of truth and love have always won. There have been tyrants ..., but in the end, they always fall."
—Mahatma Gandhi

3 things I am grateful for today:	A Note of Love for...
1).	
2).	
3).	

Date: _____   **Time:** _____

"'Enough' is a feast." (Buddhist proverb)
"Enough is as good as a feast." (Sir Thomas Malory)

3 things I am grateful for today:	A Note of Love for...
1).	
2).	
3).	

"Thankfulness is the beginning of gratitude. Gratitude is the completion of thankfulness."
—Henri Frederic Amiel

3 things I am grateful for today:	A Note of Love for...
1).	
2).	
3).	

"Thankfulness may consist merely of words. Gratitude is shown in acts."
—Henri Frederic Amiel

3 things I am grateful for today:	A Note of Love for...
1).	
2).	
3).	

Date: _____   **Time:** _____

"Mercy unto you, and peace, and love, be multiplied."
(*Holy Bible*, Jude 1:2 / King James Version)

3 things I am grateful for today:	A Note of Love for...
1).	
2).	
3).	

Date: _____ **Time:** _____

"Continue in prayer, and watch in the same with thanksgiving."
(*Holy Bible*, Colossians 4:2 / King James Version)

3 things I am grateful for today:	A Note of Love for...
1).	
2).	
3).	

Date: _____   **Time:** _____

"This is my commandment, that ye love one another, as I have loved you."
(*Holy Bible*, John 15:12 / King James Version)

3 things I am grateful for today:	A Note of Love for...
1).	
2).	
3).	

Date: _____   **Time:** _____

"Gratitude is a fruit of great cultivation..."
—Samuel Johnson (Sept. 20, 1773)

3 things I am grateful for today:	A Note of Love for...
1).	
2).	
3).	

Date: _____ **Time:** _____

"They do not love that do not show their love."
—William Shakespeare (*The Two Gentlemen of Verona*, Act I, Scene 2)

3 things I am grateful for today:	A Note of Love for...
1).	
2).	
3).	

"Thankfulness is the tune of angels."
—Edmund Spenser

3 things I am grateful for today:	A Note of Love for...
1).	
2).	
3).	

Date: _____ **Time:** _____

"Hatred stirreth up strifes: but love covereth all sins."
(*Holy Bible*, Proverbs 10:12 / King James Version)

3 things I am grateful for today:	A Note of Love for...
1).	
2).	
3).	

Date: _____   **Time:** _____

"The essence of all beautiful art, all great art, is gratitude."
—Friedrich Nietzsche

3 things I am grateful for today:	A Note of Love for...
1).	
2).	
3).	

"Those who believe and do good deeds — the Gracious God will create love in their hearts."
(Holy Qur'an 19:97)

3 things I am grateful for today:	A Note of Love for...
1).	
2).	
3).	

Date: _____   **Time:** _____

"Love is the energy of life… Take away love and our earth is a tomb."
—Robert Browning

3 things I am grateful for today:	A Note of Love for...
1).	
2).	
3).	

Date: _____   **Time:** _____

"Who so loves believes the impossible."
—Elizabeth Browning

3 things I am grateful for today:	A Note of Love for...
1).	
2).	
3).	

"In your light I learn how to love."
—Rumi

3 things I am grateful for today:	A Note of Love for...
1).	
2).	
3).	

Date: _____   Time: _____

"At all times, love a friend, for he is born a brother for adversity."
(*Holy Tanakh* - Proverbs 17:17)

3 things I am grateful for today:	A Note of Love for...
1).	
2).	
3).	

"I can no other answer make, but, thanks, and thanks."
—William Shakespeare (*Twelfth Night*, Act III, Scene 3)

3 things I am grateful for today:	A Note of Love for...
1).	
2).	
3).	

"But speaking the truth in love, may grow up into him in all things ..."
(*Holy Bible*, Ephesians 4:15 / King James Version)

3 things I am grateful for today:	A Note of Love for...
1).	
2).	
3).	

Date: _____ **Time:** _____

"The minute I heard my first love story, I started looking for you..."
—Rumi

3 things I am grateful for today:	A Note of Love for...
1).	
2).	
3).	

Date: _____   **Time:** _____

"And thou shalt love the Lord thy God with all thy heart, and with all thy soul, and with all thy mind, and with all thy strength..."
(*Holy Bible*, Mark 12:30 / King James Version)

3 things I am grateful for today:	A Note of Love for...
1).	
2).	
3).	

"Gratitude to gratitude always gives birth."
—Sophocles

3 things I am grateful for today:	A Note of Love for...
1).	
2).	
3).	

Date: _____   **Time:** _____

"Greater love hath no man than this, that a man lay down his life for his friends."
(*Holy Bible*, John 15:13 / King James Version)

3 things I am grateful for today:	A Note of Love for...
1).	
2).	
3).	

Date: _____   **Time:** _____

"Gratitude is not only the greatest of virtues, but the parent of all the others."
—Cicero

3 things I am grateful for today:	A Note of Love for...
1).	
2).	
3).	

"Be devoted to one another in love. Honor one another above yourselves."
(*Holy Bible*, Romans 12:10 / New International Version)

3 things I am grateful for today:	A Note of Love for...
1).	
2).	
3).	

"We ought always to thank God for you, brothers and sisters, […] because […]
the love you have for one another is increasing."
(*Holy Bible*, 2 Thessalonians 1:3 / New International Version)

3 things I am grateful for today:	A Note of Love for...
1).	
2).	
3).	

"And the Lord make you to increase and abound in love one toward another, and toward all men, even as we do toward you."
(*Holy Bible*, 1 Thessalonians 3:12 / King James Version)

3 things I am grateful for today:	A Note of Love for...
1).	
2).	
3).	

Date: _____   **Time:** _____

"Be grateful for whoever comes, because each has been sent as a guide from beyond."
—Rumi

3 things I am grateful for today:	A Note of Love for...
1).	
2).	
3).	

Date: _____ **Time:** _____

"And the second is like unto it, Thou shalt love thy neighbour as thyself."
(*Holy Bible*, Matthew 22:39 / King James Version)

3 things I am grateful for today:	A Note of Love for...
1).	
2).	
3).	

Date: _____   **Time:** _____

"Let never day nor night unhallow'd pass, But still remember what the Lord hath done."
—William Shakespeare (*Henry VI*, Part II, Act II, scene 1)

3 things I am grateful for today:	A Note of Love for...
1).	
2).	
3).	

Date: _____   **Time:** _____

"I love the Lord, because he hath heard my voice and my supplications…He hath inclined his ear unto me, therefore will I call upon him as long as I live."
(*Holy Bible*, Psalm 116: 1-2 / King James Version)

3 things I am grateful for today:	A Note of Love for...
1).	
2).	
3).	

Date: _____ **Time:** _____

"When you arise in the morning, give thanks for the morning light, for your life and strength. Give thanks for your food, and the joy of living."
—Tecumseh, Shawnee Chief

3 things I am grateful for today:	A Note of Love for...
1).	
2).	
3).	

"That their hearts might be comforted, being knit together in love..."
(*Holy Bible*, Colossians 2:2 / King James Version)

3 things I am grateful for today:	A Note of Love for...
1).	
2).	
3).	

Date: _____ Time: _____

"Ingratitude calls forth reproaches as gratitude brings renewed kindnesses."
—Marie de Rabutin-Chantal, marquise de Sévigné, *Lettres.*

3 things I am grateful for today:	A Note of Love for...
1).	
2).	
3).	

Date: _____   Time: _____

"If ye love me, keep my commandments."
(*Holy Bible*, John 14:15 / King James Version)

3 things I am grateful for today:	A Note of Love for...
1).	
2).	
3).	

Date: _____ **Time:** _____

"As we express our gratitude, we must never forget that the highest appreciation is not to utter words, but to live by them."
—John F. Kennedy

3 things I am grateful for today:	A Note of Love for...
1).	
2).	
3).	

Date: _____   **Time:** _____

"You, my brothers and sisters, were called to be free. But do not use your freedom to indulge the flesh; rather, serve one another humbly in love."
(*Holy Bible*, Galatians 5:13 / New International Version)

3 things I am grateful for today:	A Note of Love for...
1).	
2).	
3).	

Date: _____ **Time:** _____

"Be thankful to God: whoever gives thanks benefits his own soul..."
(*Holy Qur'an* 31:12 / Abdul Haleem translation)

3 things I am grateful for today:	A Note of Love for...
1).	
2).	
3).	

Date: _____ **Time:** _____

"Love is the beauty of the soul."
—Saint Augustine

3 things I am grateful for today:	A Note of Love for...
1).	
2).	
3).	

"So remember Me; I will remember you. Be thankful to Me, and never ungrateful."
(*Holy Qur'an* 2:152 / Abdul Haleem translation)

3 things I am grateful for today:	A Note of Love for...
1).	
2).	
3).	

Date: _____ **Time:** _____

"Love is the only force capable of transforming an enemy into a friend."
—Martin Luther King

3 things I am grateful for today:	A Note of Love for...
1).	
2).	
3).	

Date: _____   **Time:** _____

"They shall give thanks to the Lord for His kindness, and for His wonders to the children of men."

(*Holy Tanakh* - Psalms 107:15)

3 things I am grateful for today:	A Note of Love for...
1).	
2).	
3).	

"You yourself, as much as anybody in the entire universe, deserve your love and affection."
—Mahatma Gandhi

3 things I am grateful for today:	A Note of Love for...
1).	
2).	
3).	

Date: _____   **Time:** _____

"Give thanks to the Lord, for He is good, for His loving-kindness is eternal."
(*Holy Tanakh* - II Chronicles - Chapter 7:3)

3 things I am grateful for today:	A Note of Love for...
1).	
2).	
3).	

Date: _____   **Time:** _____

"How do I love thee? Let me count the ways."
—Elizabeth Browning

3 things I am grateful for today:	A Note of Love for...
1).	
2).	
3).	

"So, fall asleep love, loved by me."
—Robert Browning

3 things I am grateful for today:	A Note of Love for...
1).	
2).	
3).	

Date: _____ **Time:** _____

"Reflect upon your present blessings — of which every man has many — not on your past misfortunes, of which all men have some."
— Charles Dickens (*A Christmas Carol*)

3 things I am grateful for today:	A Note of Love for...
1).	
2).	
3).	

Date: _____ **Time:** _____

"So God gave them the reward of this world and the good reward of the Hereafter. And God loves those who do good."
(*Holy Qur'an* 3:148 / Abdul Haleem translation)

3 things I am grateful for today:	A Note of Love for...
1).	
2).	
3).	

"Many waters cannot quench the love, nor can rivers flood it..."
(*Holy Tanakh* - Song of Songs 8:7)

3 things I am grateful for today:	A Note of Love for...
1).	
2).	
3).	

Date: _____ **Time:** _____

"O Lord that lends me life, Lend me a heart replete with thankfulness!"
—William Shakespeare (*Henry VI*, Part Two, Act I, Scene 1)

3 things I am grateful for today:	A Note of Love for...
1).	
2).	
3).	

"And this commandment have we from him, That he who loveth God love his brother also."

(*Holy Bible*, 1 John 4:21 / King James Version)

3 things I am grateful for today:	A Note of Love for...
1).	
2).	
3).	

"He is a wise man who does not grieve for the things which he has not, but rejoices for those which he has."
—Epictetus

3 things I am grateful for today:	A Note of Love for...
1).	
2).	
3).	

Date: _____   **Time:** _____

"Yet the Lord will command his lovingkindness in the day time, and in the night his song shall be with me, and my prayer unto the God of my life."
(*Holy Bible*, Psalm 42:8 / King James Version)

3 things I am grateful for today:	A Note of Love for...
1).	
2).	
3).	

"Well then, if ever I thank any man, I'll thank you."
—William Shakespeare (*As You Like It*, Act II Scene 5)

3 things I am grateful for today:	A Note of Love for...
1).	
2).	
3).	

Date: _____   **Time:** _____

"He that hath my commandments, and keepeth them, he it is that loveth me: and he that loveth me shall be loved of my Father, and I will love him."
(*Holy Bible*, John 14:21 / King James Version)

3 things I am grateful for today:	A Note of Love for...
1).	
2).	
3).	

Date: _____   **Time:** _____

"If you see no reason for giving thanks, the fault lies with yourself."
—Tecumseh, Shawnee Chief

3 things I am grateful for today:	A Note of Love for...
1).	
2).	
3).	

Date: _____   **Time:** _____

"Let brotherly love continue. Be not forgetful to entertain strangers: for thereby some have entertained angels unawares."
(*Holy Bible*, Hebrews 13:1-2 / King James Version)

3 things I am grateful for today:	A Note of Love for...
1).	
2).	
3).	

Date: _____ **Time:** _____

"Thou thought'st to help me; and such thanks I give
As one near death to those that wish him live."
—William Shakespeare (*All's Well That Ends Well,* Act II, Scene 1)

3 things I am grateful for today:	A Note of Love for...
1).	
2).	
3).	

Date: _____   **Time:** _____

"For this is the message that ye heard from the beginning, that we should love one another."

(*Holy Bible*, 1 John 3:11 / King James Version)

3 things I am grateful for today:	A Note of Love for...
1).	
2).	
3).	

"Give thanks to the Lord, for He is good, for His loving-kindness is eternal."
—(*Holy Tanakh* - II Chronicles 7:3)

3 things I am grateful for today:	A Note of Love for...
1).	
2).	
3).	

"For he that will love life, and see good days, let him refrain his tongue [...], and [...] speak no guile: Let him [...] do good; let him seek peace, and ensue it."
(*Holy Bible*, 1 Peter 3:10-11 / King James Version)

3 things I am grateful for today:	A Note of Love for...
1).	
2).	
3).	

Date: _____ **Time:** _____

"Lovers don't finally meet somewhere. They're in each other all along."
—Rumi

3 things I am grateful for today:	A Note of Love for...
1).	
2).	
3).	

Date: _____   **Time:** _____

"But thanks be to God, which giveth us the victory through our Lord..."
(*Holy Bible*, 1 Corinthians 15:57 / King James Version)

3 things I am grateful for today:	A Note of Love for...
1).	
2).	
3).	

"I have decided to stick with love. Hate is too great a burden to bear."
—Martin Luther King, Jr.

3 things I am grateful for today:	A Note of Love for...
1).	
2).	
3).	

"He that loveth not knoweth not God, for God is love."
(*Holy Bible*, 1 John 4:8 / King James Version)

3 things I am grateful for today:	A Note of Love for...
1).	
2).	
3).	

Date: _____ **Time:** _____

"Love is a serious mental disease... Be kind, for everyone you meet is fighting a hard battle."
—Plato

3 things I am grateful for today:	A Note of Love for...
1).	
2).	
3).	

Date: _____   Time: _____

"Let us always meet each other with a smile, for the smile is the beginning of love."
—Mother Teresa

3 things I am grateful for today:	A Note of Love for...
1).	
2).	
3).	

Date: _____   **Time:** _____

"And let the peace of God rule in your hearts, to the which also ye are called in one body; and be ye thankful."
(*Holy Bible*, Colossians 3:15 / King James Version)

3 things I am grateful for today:	A Note of Love for...
1).	
2).	
3).	

Date: _____   Time: _____

"Love the sinner and hate the sin."
—Saint Augustine

3 things I am grateful for today:	A Note of Love for...
1).	
2).	
3).	

"Your task is not to seek for love, but merely to seek and find all the barriers within yourself that you have built against it."
—Rumi

3 things I am grateful for today:	A Note of Love for...
1).	
2).	
3).	

"Rejoice evermore. Pray without ceasing. In every thing give thanks."
(*Holy Bible*, 1 Thessalonians 5:16-18 / King James Version)

3 things I am grateful for today:	A Note of Love for...
1).	
2).	
3).	

Date: _____   **Time:** _____

"The measure of love is to love without measure."
—Saint Augustine

3 things I am grateful for today:	A Note of Love for...
1).	
2).	
3).	

"I will praise thee, O Lord, with my whole heart; I will shew forth all thy marvellous works."
(*Holy Bible*, Psalm 9:1 / King James Version)

3 things I am grateful for today:	A Note of Love for...
1).	
2).	
3).	

Date: _____ **Time:** _____

"Let the peace of Christ rule in your hearts, since as members of one body you were called to peace. And be thankful."
(*Holy Bible*, Colossians 3:15 / New International Version)

3 things I am grateful for today:	A Note of Love for...
1).	
2).	
3).	

Date: _____   **Time:** _____

"At the touch of love everyone becomes a poet."
—Plato

3 things I am grateful for today:	A Note of Love for...
1).	
2).	
3).	

"Be careful for nothing; but in every thing by prayer and supplication with thanksgiving let your requests be made known unto God."
(*Holy Bible*, Philippians 4:6-7 / King James Version)

3 things I am grateful for today:	A Note of Love for...
1).	
2).	
3).	

"To fall in love with God is the greatest romance; to seek him the greatest adventure; to find him, the greatest human achievement."
—Saint Augustine

3 things I am grateful for today:	A Note of Love for...
1).	
2).	
3).	

Date: _____   **Time:** _____

"O give thanks unto the Lord; for he is good; for his mercy endureth for ever."
(*Holy Bible*, 1 Chronicles 16:34 / King James Version)

3 things I am grateful for today:	A Note of Love for...
1).	
2).	
3).	

Date: _____ **Time:** _____

> *"The course of true love never did run smooth."*
> —William Shakespeare (*A Midsummer Night's Dream,* Act I Scene 1)

3 things I am grateful for today:	A Note of Love for...
1).	
2).	
3).	

"What does love look like? It has the hands to help others. It has the feet to hasten to the poor and needy. It has eyes to see misery and want. It has the ears to hear the sighs and sorrows of men. That is what love looks like."

—Saint Augustine